This One's For You

Joanne Nuque

BookLeaf
Publishing

Presentation by *BookLeaf Publishing*

Web: www.bookleafpub.com

E-mail: info@bookleafpub.com

ISBN: 978-93-95950-53-4

First edition 2022

To all fledgling writers both young and old,

Your words are every bit as important as everyone else's.

ACKNOWLEDGEMENT

Many thanks to Joy Valenzuela for encouraging me to write this book, and my friends, especially my best friend, Neryl Anne Denosta, for cheering me on as I wrote these poems.
A hundred thank-yous to Jullia Granada for designing this book's beautiful cover.
And of course, I'd like to thank Benjamin Gharachorloo, my lovely fiancé who never grows tired of reading anything I write, no matter how terrible it may be.

Contents

You

All my life had been spent searching for you.

You, I first caught, that moment in sixth grade, born from a pair of childish minds, the story of two rabbits, children, like I was, sowing chaos in a school of animals.

Then came the still, solitary evenings after school, streaks of you colouring the empty document, to be shared with by a kind friend.

You left behind a mysterious forest of black roses, a mountain to look upon the entire world, a pair of mischievous witches on a journey for jokes. I watched a lifelong friendship burgeon from you.

I knew you since the seventh grade, from the assignment where I had to write what I wanted to be when I grew up. I knew you well, saw you every day. I wasn't afraid to say so and declared it. And They didn't mind; in fact, They loved you and smiled. I was young.

Then, I lost sight of you in high school, the pressures of the future, the tugs from family, duty, and career, burying you beneath the textbooks, the math, the science of impending adulthood. I could not know you.

To know you was to fail.

And so, I ignored you and your persistent calls, placed you in a box, and slid you to the furthest reaches of my closet floor, bundled behind the old sweaters I outgrew and forgot.

Sometimes, however, I'd catch glimpses of you.

The odd afternoons free of responsibility, the long hot showers before bed, the few hours in the night spent sequestered in my room with the laptop rested on my thighs, the white glare of the screen reflected in the lenses of my gawkish glasses.

You came to me as the young wizard girl watching a revolution unfold through her father, the shy barista boy at the subway station café pining for a friend, a moody murderer on the mend, the petulant office drone seeking adventure in a world of dreary automation.

Then, I rejected you in university. You asked me to give you a chance, but I could not take that risk.

You were not scholarly enough. You were not handsome with a career that would loft you further up the ladder of life. You were not wise or mature or sophisticated. Not dependable or traditional.

No, you were naïve, silly, a mistake, a poor planner, a consequence of indolence, a deceitful wooer that whispered sweet nothings into my ear and beckoned me to waste away at the keyboard.

But I loved you.

And your words weren't sweet nothings. Your words were everything.

I lived for you.

After graduation, I had lost sight of me. All I knew were what They wanted of me, of where They told me I should go. And I listened. I obeyed. And I searched all day and night for something that wasn't you but resembled you, so that I may appease Them. Fruitlessly, I scoured.

Then, the days passed. The seasons, too. The years. And I grew hopeless and old. I could not be like the rest of Them, who ascended to greater worlds. I could not find what They told me to find.

Stifled by the mundanity of my life, I went to you for solace every chance I had. On my lonely breaks in the lunchroom, my fingers gliding over the keyboard of my phone, you wishing I were elsewhere. On the sleepy bus rides to work, the blue expanse of sky as bright and boundless and so full of potential as you. On the walks home from the train station, the orange sun setting over the crags of ruddy rooftops, the asphalt warm beneath my feet, you, again, whispering secrets in my ear, pulling smiles from my taut lips like a magician pulls the impossible from a black hat.

I'd find you in bits and pieces of my lover. With him, you birthed a hero of sun, dictated the flow of her odyssey to save the world, grew from roots her life, her family, her friends, her lover, and blossomed a field of yellow carnations in a world of black and white institutions.

You dwelled in my lover's basement, kindled by the warmth of the fireplace, the coziness his refuge brought us at a time when entire cities emptied, and everyone retreated into their homes for fear of a pervasive sickness.

Then, my lover confessed that the smile illuminating my face whenever I spoke of you was a smile that knew the ripest of joys, the pride of hard work, the freedom from which passion piggybacks. He said whenever you came to me, I was radiant. I was the sun.

Then, it all clicked, and the dawn burst through the clouds, blazed the horizon.

In the first time since childhood, I saw you. Really saw you. And I acknowledged you, took your hand, shook it, and embraced you. Then, I fell to my knees, wept tears of sorrow, from years lost and spent missing you, but also from joy, because to finally know you is to know myself.

All my life had been spent searching for you.

I forgot I already carried you in the crevices of my brain, the lines on my hands, the red veins in my eyes. I pushed you away for so long, was always guilty after our brief trysts.

But no more. I accept you now, and I'll cherish you forever, for as long as you'll have me. Because you are magic. You are inspiration. You are love, and light, and longing.

Today, you brought me a boy of many troubles thrusted into a world of many faces.

I wonder, who will you bring me, where will you take me, tomorrow? What else will you whisper into my ear?

Stillness

a homebody
gazes through the window
soaring through cumulonimbus clouds
into a sea of fog
pungent with ginkgo

a homebody
draws arcs of lightning on the glass
glimpses the faint lights of towers pass
hears the pitter patter of cold rain
sees the sluice streaming down the panes

a homebody
sits to soothe
and sits to write
observes the moon ascend
the sun alight

Head

Captivity and doldrums
Birth breathing worlds in my head

For as long as I can remember
I write to make my characters
Live the lives I cannot live

Windows

For most of my life, I've looked out windows,
At eight stories high, a parking lot of faded
beat-up cars,
A noisy highway behind it backed up with
speeding cars
At three stories high, a sickly green soccer field,
and a rank schoolyard,
With sloping hills and branchy trees, fences of
grey bars

For most of my life, I've been confined,
Sheltered within my room's four walls,
Longing to go, waiting to flee,
But knowing if I do, questions then loom
Where will I go? What will I be?

Habits are a hard thing to shatter,
When fear is what you're taught,
Fear is all that matters

And now I am here
In a steel glass tower
Twenty-three floors
City skyline views
Drenched in rain shower

At least from here
I can see the world
More people, more places
More lives to observe
Planes overhead
Soar past unheard

Oyster I

The world is not your oyster
Even though they say it is
The world is the oyster they want you to
become,
The soldier who marches not to the beat of their
own drum,
But to the beat of the status quo
Oh woe
Is us,
An overgrown garden
With weeds and seeds of motley annuals
Beautiful and untethered, flourishing by the
hour, the year, the seasons
Only to be trimmed and manicured to
Their liking
Sculpted to be
Their brand of striking
Hear only their reasons
Excuses
Reduce us, but that's okay
Because we'll listen anyway
Because that's how we were raised
It's hard to be yourself in a world so torn apart
Where zombies shuffle around, gloomy circles
under their eyes

Brittle
And dazed
You keep going because there is no other way
To stop is to fail is to die the worst way

Panic

Blinding explosions behind my eyes
Ears ringing, deafened, no surprise
Like tempests thrashing the window glass,
The sudden deluge of vines attacks,
How quickly it comes, how long it stays,
Like peering into the monster's gaze
I cannot talk, I cannot think,
I want to run, but I just sink
Clawing, dragging, the pressure crests
The feeling grinds hard in my chest,
A log caught in a wild whirlpool,
The voices reverberate their ridicule,
I am so tired, I am so scared,
To others, my insecurities bared

Hard

There is nothing but static in my head
When the floodgates fly open
The only way to handle it
Is to pretend that I am dead

I know, I know
That's not the way to do it
To get better is to move forward
To get better is to come forward
About what lies under the border
Of thought and tongue
And eye and lung
And there's only so much time
That your heart is young

But I'm aware of all of this
And still it's hard to change
I feel like my ways are cemented
I feel like I can't rearrange
The pieces of me
To build a better person
Or at least a normal person
That can go through life
The way I'm supposed to go

Get a proper job, make money
Get a proper house, make my family,
Grow old, grow tired
Die after I retire

It's depressing, right?
No, I'm just making it depressing
Life is what you make it
That's what they say
But life is also hard
And that's just the way
It is, right?
Will I make it out alright?

Doors

Why do I have so much trouble opening doors
Figuratively, but literally too
Why is it so hard to pick out what I want
To eat, to wear, to watch every day
And why do I talk to adults
As if I myself am not one
And when will I feel like I am

Also what more will I need to do
To stop feeling like
I'm walking side by side with giants all the time

Can you tell me the formula
For growing up
Please, I don't want to mess this up

Mud

I am stuck in squat sludge
Stiff, sloppy, syrupy, solid
I squirm, I shift, I stir, I slip
I sob, I scream, I stomp, I spit
I shrivel

I am stuck
I set
I am sacrificed
I submit
To the slabs of slush
To the smears of scum and slime
Where I spoil in sour stenches

Slip through cracks into the soil and silt
Slog through the swamps for something
To sustain me some day

Sometimes, all I starve for is
Stillness and serenity

Pure

How great it would be
To swirl down the drain
And disappear for free
Dirty water washed away
Cleansed and scrubbed
I'll find a way
To be pure again

Like the leaves that die in autumn
Like the grass that grows anew
Like the spring flowers that will blossom
To begin again, I'll pursue

Just as skies will always blacken, then lighten,
then glow
Just as winters summon darkness, coldness, and
snow
The path is flushed with shadows, and streams
of sunlight too
And from this long and hard journey, there's one
thing I'll learn to do
Move forward on this path with a gentle kind of
brightness
Gathering hope, resilience, tenderness, and
kindness

Brother

Cheesepuffs and rollerblading in circles around
the living room
Your egregious purple toe, the dead nail that
wilted and tumbled off
Remember the time the doorknob smashed your
head?
Remember the time you nearly drowned in the
deep end?
Our cartoons and Pokémon, Beyblade, and
Bakugan
Our favourite video games: Street Fighters and
Super Smash Bros

Remember the summer afternoons so hot and
humid?
You on your long board, us on our bikes
The streets blending in with the sky, the blacktop
melting
The soft serve ice cream, the sun on our skin
The First of July
Fireworks through shadowy criss-crossing arms
of oak trees in the park
Lights tore the black night with brilliant reds and
whites

And I chased you down a flower lined trail,
shadows nipping at your head

Remember the places of our youth?
The murky brown rivers
The grassy dragonfly fields
The train tracks with the dog skull
Roaming asphalt roads
Wheelies beneath buzzing telephone wires
Cresting hills and playground gyms
The tracks of our scooter tires

Remember long summer drives anywhere?
The mountain and the mountain air
Barbecue, hotdogs, and smores by the lake
For your birthday, a DQ chocolate ice cream
cake

Then Fall came and you retreated
To a den you had completed
And summer's come and gone
Many summers have come and gone
And you've yet to make your reappearance
And slowly, I'm forgetting
Your face, your voice, your smile, your laughter
Our games, our songs, our drives, our chatter
I miss you
We miss you
We really do

But Brother, know that I will wait for you
Every summer, every dawn, every dusk
I'll always be here for you
Whenever you choose to return to us
And Brother, I'll always love you
Blue skies and black
Even if you don't
Want to come back

Forgiveness

It took me a long time to learn
That the words that hurled from her tongue
That the worries that seeped from her face to
mine
That the endless gulf stretched between him and
me
That the cold shoulders and silent dinners
The years we spent in the same house
Separated by walls
Was not my fault
And it wasn't even really theirs
They were as hurt and broken as me
And we weren't the first to
Grow up that way

I forgive you

Then

The walk along the lake on a late summer's
afternoon,
Despite the sun's soft rays of light dancing over
the waves,
There's a darkness in the water, a sense of
forebodingness.
My feet sink into the damp, cold sand,
But your hand feels warm in mine,
And we walk and we talk
About just anything.
We're as free as the seagulls soaring above us.

The cool breeze tousles my hair,
And you brush it out of my eyes.
Your touch lingers on my cheek a little longer
than usual.
I'll miss this, I think as I try to memorize the
way your lips curve into that beautiful smile of
yours,
The way your hazel eyes light up when you talk
about the future.
You are the epitome of love and warmth and
home.
I can't imagine going through the long day
without hearing your voice.

At the end of the stretch of sand we stop.
"I'll be over there next month" you say, pointing
across the lake,
Dozens of miles away.
The city skyline dots the horizon,
Skyscrapers in a line, glimmering steel, bob over
evermoving, glassy waves.
A sudden sadness coils in my stomach and I try
my best to smile,
But you see it doesn't quite reach my
shimmering eyes.

"Don't worry, this is for our future," you tell me
"Just picture this: in a couple years' time,
us, our dogs, and a house."
Your hand squeezes mine,
And your smile is reassuring,
And without warning you embrace me
wholeheartedly,
Lifting me up and twirling me around.
Laughter fills the air and I sink into this joy, let
it capture me.

"And don't forget Melon" I tease.
She's the conure you named,
Who loathes you but loves me.
Your smile never falters, "Yes, and Melon."

Learning

You asked me,
"How should I love you?
How should I be there for you?"
And I gave you
A vague answer
That you did not like
Nor understood.
In truth,
I do not know what to tell you,
Because I do not know
How to love myself
And be there for myself
In the first place.
But I still want you,
And if you'll have me,
Can we
Figure out these things together?

Love

I have loved you since the second grade
The day you came to school, the new kid
A head of curly gold brown hair and a smile that
the stars envied
After a tour of the playground, we became fast
friends
And in the eighth grade, I knew I really, really
liked you
And how you were so kind and brave and funny
and smart
And so, so tender

When you asked me out in the eleventh grade
I could hardly believe it
I didn't believe I could be loved
Didn't believe I deserved love
We were just kids
But you were determined
To show this young girl otherwise
Who knew a little blue elephant would come to
mean so much

And you and I, we were so different
Histories, mindsets, personality
You opened the world

You showed me the world
And ways of living I'd never thought were for
me

Everything that came from you, was brimming
with goodness
You sprouted life, sprung forth gardens of
wildflowers
Enticed birds, bees, and everything in between
And dreams clouded your head, and moved into
mine

I'd lie awake in bed wondering
How could he be mine
How could I have a love
How could he want to stay
When I have holes in my head
And cracks running down my skin
When I am fractured
And my emotions pour and pour and pour
And beat down on everyone around me

How can you love me
When I am so beneath you
You've got the peaks of mountains in sight
And I can only see my feet on concrete

How can you love me
When you do so much

And I can only offer you crumbs
A trade that isn't ever fair
For you
How will I ever be good enough
For you
How could you not want more

Even now, newly engaged
I have doubts that you'll leave me
People usually leave me
And I don't want to be alone

But eight years is a long time
And every year you're still by my side
And every year you renew in me
This feeling of us
This feeling of it's just meant to be
Don't jinx it, let it be
Enjoy it, enjoy us
This is what he's taught me
Love and how to love me
Life and how to just be

You make me believe
We'll make it together

How patient, how kind
How loving you are

My guiding light, my best friend
My wish upon a field of stars
I love you

Now

Seasons have passed and now we live together,
Miraculously so.
Moved out, made a home, we are on our own.
Freedom clings to the curls of your hair,
The strands of mine.
My body exudes sunshine,
And your presence brings the cool relief of a
summer breeze,
And we leave blooms in the wake of our feet,
And our apartment is jungly with them.
And Melon is content to perch on the branches
of our many trees.

Every morning, you lay tender beside me,
The rays of light creeping in through the glass,
Tickling your eyes awake until they flutter open
like the butterflies
I released from my tummy years ago,
The indigo ones we've tended for many
generations.

Not every day is perfect,
But with you, I am as liberated as the endless
night sky.

And if ever the thought crosses my mind,
That I am unlucky,
I remember
The stars had to have aligned,
And the cosmos must've conspired
To bring us together,
And keep us together
For all these years.

Future

I visualize the future when the present is a
formidable foe
I imagine what it's like to arc home from work
to you
The cuddles on the couch, the murmurs of a
show or movie on the screen
Or maybe we'd be playing the video game
we've waited all year to get released
Or the D&D campaign you finally prepped and
finished
This time, you'll make dinner and I'll relax and
maybe give you advice on how to cook the
salmon
This time, I can tell you all the things I did today
Because I got out of bed, got dressed, and left
the apartment
And did the adult thing of speaking to strangers,
of driving to work, of earning money for our
living
Because I did not let the storm clouds wear me
down, smother me into the bed sheets, smudge
the lines of my smile, burble all the ways I am
lacking
Because I am good enough and I can venture
into the unknown and come home unscathed,

And even if I am a little scathed, I'll heal
Because I am strong
I am strong for us
And then when we're weary, we'll get ready for
bed
I'll have my book and you'll have yours
And we'll read under the warm amber light of
the night lamp
And we'll fall asleep in each other's arms, our
legs intertwined, the pillows soft, the blankets
softer
And when we wake up in the morning, hair
disheveled and eyes sleepy but bright,
I'll still be okay
And you know I'll be alright

Sing

A long, long time ago, my family's tiny
apartment
Was the center of the universe
Family, friends, neighbours
Congregated together
To feast, to celebrate, to talk, to recreate
Sunny afternoons in the Philippines
Drink beer, play cards
Chatter and song filled my ears
Titas and lolas pinched my ears
And cooed
And I was loved
Days then
Feel like a lifetime ago

In some ways they were
I was only a small child
And now I am full grown
And I wonder where did those family friends go
One day, they just upped and vanished
Mom and Dad did not panic
First friends, then extended family
I grew up, focused on our family
Instilled in me the mindset
"Those outside us are a big threat

To our safety and our happiness
We don't need friends
When we have each other
We are stronger when together"

But I grew
And learned it wasn't true
I grew and lived a life of solitude
Four walls, a window
And layers of bricks between us
A fear of people
A fear of trust
What a lonely life it was
For me, for them
I wonder if they miss
Those parties, those nights
Their kith, their kin

We became a quiet family
I became a quiet girl
But as I did my growing
I made friends, I unfurled
In front of them
Let them in
Went through school and love
And work and life together
Shared trauma, sobbed in each other's arms
Smiled and laughed together

But for a year, I went dormant
Ignored them
Curled inward
A time when my insecurities
Whispered fresh anxieties
Into my ears
When I longed to hear
The chatter and song
I thought
Why would they care about me
I am not important
I have always been an outsider
Making friendships was inadvertent
I don't need friends
When I have my family
My lover and my books
This is all I need to be happy
I am safe, I am—

Crappy

I missed my confidants,
Long talks, long walks
Sleepovers and food
Parties and destinations
Going, going, going
Our youth
Freedom never tasted
So sweet, so good

My best friend, I love her
Brought me back from a dark world
Some people don't get second chances
But here I was with an oyster
In the palm of my hands

Now I've just had one of the best summers of
my life
The chatter, the song, it all rushed back
I've never sang so loud, never seen lights so
bright
And I'll never stop singing
With them at my side
Blue skies, this life

Oyster II

The world is your oyster
It's true what I say
You can be who you want to become,
A revolutionary marching to the beat of their
own drum
To beat down the status quo
Oh woe
Is them,
Fearful of a vibrant garden
With sprouts and seeds of motley wildflowers
Frightened by our beauty, we flourish by the
hour, the year, the seasons
Can't be trimmed or manicured to
Their liking
Can't be sculpted to be
Their brand of striking
Deaf to their reasons
Excuses
Won't reduce us, we're okay
'Cause we won't listen anyway
Go against how we were raised
We'll carve our own path in a world so torn apart
Steer clear of the zombies shuffling around
New hope
Determination

You keep going because there is no other way
To be you is to be free is to live the right way

Reminder

Life can be good
Unlearn the lesson that
Life is about waiting
For the Next Horrible Thing
Happiness doesn't necessitate guilt
Good things can happen just because
And just because good things happen
Does not mean bad things will shortly follow
You are allowed to be happy
It is your birthright as a human being

Write a list
Of all the things that make
Life worth living
Stick it on your fridge, your wall
A reminder of all things good
Happiness when night falls

Goodness will always find you
If you search for it

Me

I love you
And all that you've been through
So stubborn, but you're learning
To yield
To begin again
To take back what they've taken from you
To become you, the woman you've always
wanted to be
Not what they wanted you to be

I love you
Because you are beautiful
A plump goddess
With a long face, a big nose
Skin like butterscotch with cute smudgy spots
Eyes that glimmer like the night sky
A big teeth-baring smile that's brighter than the
sun
Thick thighs, thick limbs, fat cheeks, fat tummy
Curves in all the right places
Pudgy body, but that's okay
Because you've always been gorgeous
Because you've always been precious
And you deserve all the compliments
That come your way

I love you
Because despite all the scary things you know
you must go through
Despite all the baggage you carry from a
lifetime spent silent
You are moving forward
You will not sit and sink
You have the courage
You have the skill
You are ready
Even if you still get doubts sometimes
Even if you still cry

I love you
You are trying
To be better
To grow
To break through the boundaries of what has
been
Erected before you, generations ago
Steel walls block the sun
But you still scale
Because you keep your promises

I love you
Because you laugh and smile
And call your friends again
You are coming out of your shell

And you are glowing, absolutely radiant
You are learning to unlearn
That people aren't there to crush you by default
You are learning
That people can be kind and vulnerable like you
That people can be scared and anxious like you
That people can be beautiful and broken like you
And you have found your people
And you have made your home
And you can only soar up from here

I love you
Because you care
You worry and you fret
And it kills you
But you love
You really do
And you want wants best
For the people around you

I love you
Because you sing, you dance
You write, you learn
You try
You love
And the world is better for it
And you are wanted here
And you are needed
And you are cherished by so many people

Never forget it
You are loved